Sing alleluia!

An Easter
Alleluia

By Anita Reith Stohs

Illustrated by Joel Snyder

CONCORDIA PUBLISHING HOUSE • SAINT LOUIS

Text copyright © 2003 Anita Reith Stohs
Illustrations copyright © 2003 Concordia Publishing House
Published by Concordia Publishing House
3558 S. Jefferson Avenue, St. Louis, MO 63118-3968
Manufactured in the United States of America

2   3   4   5   6   7   8   9   10   12   11   10   09   08   07   06   05   04   03

To the memory of my father, Pastor Ferdinand Reith,

who has taken his place in the heavenly choirs.

Revelation 7:9–10

Alleluia! Let us sing

Praises to our risen King!

In our place, on Calvary,
Jesus died for you and me.

Sing alleluia,
Sing alleluia,
Sing alleluia—
He died for you and me!

Early in the morning light,
Some women saw an angel
bright.

Heard the news he had to say—
That Jesus rose on Easter Day!

Sing alleluia,
Sing alleluia,
Sing alleluia—
He rose on Easter day!

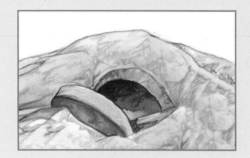

Jesus then appeared to them.

What joy they felt to see their Friend!

With happy hearts the women ran
To spread the news, "He lives again!"

Sing alleluia,
Sing alleluia,
Sing alleluia—
Our Jesus lives again!

Jesus lives and loves us so;

He goes everywhere we go.

Jesus cares for us each day,
And He hears us when we pray.

Sing alleluia,
Sing alleluia,
Sing alleluia—
He hears us when we pray!

Jesus lives and so will we

With Him in heaven eternally.

Alleluia let us sing,

Unto Jesus Christ, our King!

Sing alleluia,

Sing alleluia,

Sing alleluia

To Jesus Christ, our King!

Dear Parent,

"Alleluia" means "Praise the Lord."

During the season of Lent, our alleluias are "buried" as we focus on the sins Christ took to the cross on our behalf. At Easter the alleluias return. And like the women at the tomb on that first Easter morning, our hearts are filled with joy at the wonder of Jesus' resurrection and we become "Alleluia" people as, through the power of the Holy Spirit, the Lord of Life lives in our hearts and transforms our lives with His loving presence.

Read the story of the resurrection as found in Matthew 28:1–10 to your children. Use this book to help teach them that the good news of the angel at the tomb is their Good News today. Because Jesus took our place on the cross, our sins are forgiven. Because He lives, we have the promise of eternal life in heaven, and we have the assurance of Jesus' constant presence in our lives, knowing that He is here to guide and protect us and to hear our prayers and praise.

As you prepare for Easter, look for ways to emphasize its real meaning. Decorate eggs with Easter crosses, outlines of the open tomb, Easter angels, the word "Alleluia!" or other words from Scripture. As you decorate the eggs, talk about how the egg, from which a chick hatches to new life, has long been a Christian symbol for Jesus' resurrection. While you work, play a Christian CD or cassette or sing familiar Easter hymns and songs.

Consider making an "Alleluia Tree" by blowing eggs, decorating them with Easter symbols, and hanging them from a branch placed in a jar or can. If you cut your branch from a budding tree and place it in water, the buds will open in a few days, adding to the symbolism of the new life we have in Christ. Place your tree in a prominent part of your home to remind you of your joy that Jesus has risen.

Take time to explain to your child other symbols of Jesus' resurrection found in your home or church. Explain how the butterfly, which comes out of a dead-looking cocoon, reminds us that Jesus arose from the grave on the first Easter morning. Tell how the Easter lily, which grows from a dead-looking bulb, is also a reminder of this.

Christ is risen; He is risen indeed! Let the joy of Jesus' resurrection fill your hearts so you, like the women in the story, share the Good News of Jesus' death and resurrection with others.

Alleluia!

The author